In the Presence of Schopenhauer

In the Presence of Schopenhauer

Michel Houellebecq

Preface by Agathe Novak-Lechevalier

Translated by Andrew Brown

polity

Originally published in French as *En présence de Schopenhauer* © Michel Houellebecq and Flammarion, Paris, 2016
This edition © Polity Press, 2020

Preface by Agathe Novak-Lechevalier reprinted with permission of Éditions de l'Herne. Original title: Préface Agathe Novak-Lechevalier © Éditions de l'Herne, 2017. All rights reserved.

Reprinted 2020 (three times), 2021

Polity Press
65 Bridge Street
Cambridge CB2 1UR, UK

Polity Press
101 Station Landing
Suite 300
Medford, MA 02155, USA

ISBN-13: 978-1-5095-4324-3
ISBN-13: 978-1-5095-4325-0

A catalogue record for this book is available from the British Library.

Library of Congress Cataloging-in-Publication Data

Names: Houellebecq, Michel, author. | Brown, Andrew (Literary translator), translator.
Title: In the presence of Schopenhauer / Michel Houellebecq ; preface by Agathe Novak-Lechevalier ; translated by Andrew Brown.
Other titles: En présence de Schopenhauer. English
Description: Cambridge, UK ; Medford, MA, USA : Polity, 2020. | Summary: "An ode to Schopenhauer by one of France's most famous living authors"-- Provided by publisher.
Identifiers: LCCN 2019055829 (print) | LCCN 2019055830 (ebook) | ISBN 9781509543243 (hardback) | ISBN 9781509543250 (paperback) | ISBN 9781509543267 (epub)
Subjects: LCSH: Schopenhauer, Arthur, 1788-1860--Influence. | Houellebecq, Michel--Philosophy.
Classification: LCC B3148 .H6313 2020 (print) | LCC B3148 (ebook) | DDC 193--dc23
LC record available at https://lccn.loc.gov/2019055829
LC ebook record available at https://lccn.loc.gov/2019055830

Typeset in 10.25 on 16.5 pt Plantin MT
by Fakenham Prepress Solutions, Fakenham, Norfolk NR21 8NL
Printed and bound in the United States by LSC Communications

The publisher has used its best endeavours to ensure that the URLs for external websites referred to in this book are correct and active at the time of going to press. However, the publisher has no responsibility for the websites and can make no guarantee that a site will remain live or that the content is or will remain appropriate.

Every effort has been made to trace all copyright holders, but if any have been overlooked the publisher will be pleased to include any necessary credits in any subsequent reprint or edition.

For further information on Polity, visit our website:
politybooks.com

Contents

Preface:
The history of a revolution

When, in 2005, Michel Houellebecq began this translation of and commentary on Schopenhauer's work
– an arduous and somewhat surprising enterprise
for Houellebecq, and one which alone testifies to the
strength of his admiration – he had just finished writing
The Possibility of an Island.[1] He devoted a few weeks
to this new project, and initially thought of turning it
into a book; then, rather quickly, he abandoned it. But
he had in the meantime translated and commented on
almost thirty extracts from two of the most famous
works by Schopenhauer (1788–1860), *The World as Will
and Representation*,[2] and 'Aphorisms on the Wisdom of
Life'.[3] The former, the philosopher's main work, was also

the work of a whole lifetime: the young Schopenhauer, who had just defended his thesis, worked intensely on it from 1814 to 1818, and a first version appeared in 1819; but he continued to add to it, and the work grew with successive editions until it became the imposing tome, often published in several volumes, which we know today. However, it was only with the publication of *Parerga and Paralipomena* (1851), where he brought together various essays (including the 'Aphorisms on the Wisdom of Life') setting out the essential points of his doctrine, that Schopenhauer finally – very late in life – found the public success he had always hoped for: 'The comedy of my celebrity begins', he is supposed to have said, 'what am I to do with it now that my hair is grey?'

In the Presence of Schopenhauer, however, is not only a commentary: it is also the story of an encounter. At the age of around twenty-five or twenty-seven – which sets the scene in the first half of the 1980s – almost by chance, Houellebecq borrowed the 'Aphorisms on the Wisdom of Life' from a library.

At the time, I already knew Baudelaire, Dostoevsky, Lautréamont, Verlaine, almost all the Romantics; a lot of science fiction, too. I had read the Bible, Pascal's Pensées, *Clifford D. Simak's* City, *Thomas Mann's* The Magic Mountain. *I wrote poems; I already had the impression I was rereading, rather than really reading; I thought I had at least come to the end of one period in my discovery of literature. And then, in a few minutes, everything dramatically changed.*

This was a decisive shock: the young man dashed across Paris, finally getting his hands on a copy of *The World as Will and Representation* which had quite suddenly become 'the most important book in the world'; and as a result of this new reading, he says, 'everything dramatically changed'.[4]

'An author', says François, the narrator of *Submission*, 'is above all a human being, present in his books',[5] and 'only literature can give you access to a spirit from beyond the grave – a more direct, more complete, deeper access than you'd have in conversation with a friend'.[6] No doubt it is precisely this mysterious and startling sensation that Houellebecq first felt on his discovery of Schopenhauer's work; no doubt, too, it was this encounter, so decisive for him, that he wanted to share with his readers by embarking on the writing of this text, significantly entitled *In the Presence of Schopenhauer*. The strength of the revelation of Schopenhauer's work was indubitably linked to the shock of recognizing an alter ego, someone with whom you immediately realize that you are going to enjoy a long companionship. Schopenhauer, the expert in suffering, the radical pessimist, the solitary misanthrope, proved to be 'reinvigorating' reading for Houellebecq – you feel less lonely when there are two of you. Indeed, one wonders whether Houellebecq was Schopenhauerian before reading Schopenhauer – or was it this reading that turned him into the man we know? Was he already, fundamentally, 'unreconciled'[7] (with the world, with men, with life), or did Schopenhauer sow the seeds of conflict? Houellebecq already loved dogs better than he loved the human race – or should we recognize, here as elsewhere, the influence of Arthur Schopenhauer? Of course, it barely matters: we are here prying into the secrets of a long-term couple. What is certain, however, is that in 1991, the year when the first of Houellebecq's works were published, Schopenhauer was everywhere: in the (devilishly Schopenhauerian) title of his essay on Lovecraft, *Against the World, Against Life*;[8] in the very first sentence of *Rester vivant (Staying Alive)*,[9]

'The world is an unfolding suffering', which angrily recalls the Schopenhauerian axiom that 'Suffering is essential to all life';[10] and even in these astonishing (to put it mildly) lines of verses from his first collection, *La Poursuite du bonheur* (*The Pursuit of Happiness*):

> I want to think of you, Arthur Schopenhauer,
> I love you and I see you in the reflection of the windows,
> The world is a dead end and I'm an old clown
> It's cold. It's very cold. Earth, adieu.[11]

This encounter was almost love at first sight, then – but it also looks remarkably like a revolution. For Schopenhauer's philosophy, which aims to develop a 'single thought'[12] able to account for the real as a whole, in all its complexity, struck Houellebecq right from the start as a formidable operator of truth. Schopenhauer opened Houellebecq's eyes and taught him to contemplate the world as it is in itself – as entirely driven by a blind and endless 'will to live' which is the essence of all things, from inert matter to men, via plants and animals. In Schopenhauer, this 'will', foreign to the principle of reason, is the basis of the absurd and tragic character of all existence, whose sufferings are at once inevitable (because 'all willing proceeds from need, and thus from deprivation, and thus from suffering')[13] and devoid of any justification. It also explains the author's legendary pessimism. This is certainly a radical pessimism; but it is also a dynamic pessimism, since, according to Houellebecq, 'disillusion is no bad thing'.[14] And Schopenhauer, according to Nietzsche's formula in the third of his *Untimely Considerations*,[15] proves to be the best of 'educators'. His words are comparable, says Nietzsche, to those of a father instructing his son: it is 'an honest, calm, goodnatured discourse before an auditor who listens to it with love'.[16] Schopenhauer's work is a school of morality which instils into the reader the qualities of honesty, serenity and constancy which characterize its author; it is also, according to Nietzsche, a lesson in style (because morality and style are two sides of the same coin): 'Schopenhauer's rough and somewhat bear-like soul teaches us not so much to feel the absence of the suppleness and courtly charm of good French writers as to disdain it'.[17] Did Nietzsche always draw all the consequences of this? Houellebecq certainly did: it is no coincidence if he constantly replies to all those who eternally reproach him for lack of style by quoting Schopenhauer's famous saying 'the first

– and virtually the only – condition of a good style is having something to say'.[18]

As Michel Onfray has decisively shown, it is, in fact, the whole of Houellebecq's work that could be read through the filter of Schopenhauer's philosophy.[19] In both cases, suffering is taken for granted, and there is the same pessimism, the same conception of style, and even the same central emphasis on compassion as the general basis for ethics; we also find the same salvific character of aesthetic contemplation, and the same impossibility of 'being at home' in the world. Once we have observed this influence, it comes as no surprise that Houellebecq initially conceived *In the Presence of Schopenhauer* as a homage: 'I propose to show, through some of my favourite passages, why Schopenhauer's intellectual attitude remains to me a model for any future philosopher; and also why, even if you ultimately find yourself in disagreement with him, you cannot fail to be deeply grateful to him.'[20]

But the enterprise – and herein lies its strength, and one of its major interests – reveals that Houellebecq does not stick to this project: in his dense, sometimes difficult commentaries on the extracts he takes the trouble to translate himself, Schopenhauer's work appears to him to be, not so much a lesson patiently and admirably assimilated, or even a model, as a formidable machine for thinking with. Little by little, the analysis emancipates itself from the letter of the text, and what we find is the outline of an investigation into the problems posed by splatter films and the representation of pornography in art, a criticism of the philosophies of the absurd, and, a little further on, a reflection on the emergence of urban poetry, the transformations of twentieth-century art, and the 'tragedy of banality' which 'remains to be written'. A wide-ranging set of ideas is reflected in this intensely personal exercise (everything here seems singularly Houellebecquian, including his note comparing 'the life of nomads' that arises from 'need', to the 'life of tourists' that arises from 'boredom'); and this thought experiment seems already to be opening up other horizons. Thus, it is doubtless no coincidence that *In the Presence of Schopenhauer* precedes *The Map and the Territory*, which is perhaps, of all Houellebecq's novels, the most Schopenhauerian.[21]

Love stories end badly, and Houellebecq claims to have moved away from Schopenhauer 'a decade or so' after discovering him. Another encounter, with Auguste

Comte, compelled him, he says, to become a positivist, 'with a kind of disappointed enthusiasm':[22] an (inevitably) reasonable new direction for him to take, but one without any warmth, deprived of the passionate exaltation that had accompanied the discovery of Schopenhauer. The article entitled 'Approches du désarroi' ('Approaches to Disarray'), first published in 1993,[23] must date back to roughly those years. In it, Houellebecq shows Schopenhauer overtaken by the very thing that he had refused to believe in and that lies right at the heart of the positivist doctrine: the movement of history. Schopenhauer's revelation of the world as 'on the one hand existing as will (as desire, as vital impulse), and on the other hand perceived as a representation (in itself neutral, innocent, purely objective, capable as such of aesthetic reconstruction') now seems, he says, to have fizzled out. This revelation, one that Schopenhauer viewed as definitive, proves to have been defeated by the 'logic of the supermarket' that prevails in contemporary liberalism: instead of 'the total organic force obstinately striving for fulfilment' suggested by the word 'will', contemporary man only knows 'a scattering of desires' and 'a certain depression of the will'; as for representation, 'deeply infected by meaning', weakened by a permanent state of self-consciousness, it has 'lost all innocence' – undermining 'artistic and philosophical activity' at the same time as the very possibility of communication between men.[24] We then slide 'into an unhealthy, fake, utterly derisory atmosphere'.[25] History will not have saved us from pessimism, then – far from it: by ruining the foundations of Schopenhauer's philosophy, it has ultimately merely aggravated its conclusions. Does this mean that history has deprived that philosophy of any validity? To answer this question, it is enough to read the solution that Houellebecq recommends at the end of his article: 'Each individual, however, can produce in himself a sort of cold revolution, by moving for a while outside the flow of information and advertising. This is quite simple: it has never been so easy to adopt an aesthetic position towards the world: you just need to step aside.'[26] Suspend the will, be aware of the gap, actively practise being out of sync: Schopenhauer, now and forever.

Agathe Novak-Lechevalier

Schopenhauer

W.B.

Leave childhood behind, my friend, and wake up!¹

Our lives unfold in space, and time is just an inessential left-over. While I have a photographic and unnecessarily precise memory of the places where the events of my life have occurred, I can locate these events in time only as a series of contrived and approximate overlaps. So when I borrowed 'Aphorisms on the Wisdom of Life' from the municipal library of the seventh arrondissement in Paris (more specifically, its annex in the Latour-Maubourg district), I may have been aged twenty-six, but equally possibly twenty-five, or twenty-seven. In any case, this is very late in life for such a major discovery. At the time, I already knew Baudelaire, Dostoevsky, Lautréamont, Verlaine, almost all the Romantics; a lot of science fiction, too. I had read the Bible, Pascal's *Pensées*, Clifford D. Simak's *City*, Thomas Mann's *The Magic Mountain*. I wrote poems; I already had the impression

I was rereading, rather than really reading; I thought I had at least completed one period in my discovery of literature. And then, in a few minutes, everything dramatically changed.

After searching for two weeks, I managed to buy a copy of *The World as Will and Representation*, found on a shelf in the Presses Universitaires de France bookstore on the boulevard Saint-Michel; at the time, the book was available only second-hand (for months I expressed my surprise aloud, I must have told dozens of people about my astonishment: here we were in Paris, one of the main European capitals, and the most important book in the world had not even been reissued!). In philosophy, I had barely gone beyond Nietzsche, where, in fact, I got more or less stuck. I found his philosophy immoral and repulsive, but his intellectual power impressed me. I would have liked to destroy Nietzscheanism, to tear it down to its very foundations, but I did not know how to do so; intellectually, I was floored. Needless to say, it was here again my reading of Schopenhauer that changed everything. I've even stopped bearing poor Nietzsche a grudge; he had the misfortune to come after Schopenhauer, that's all – just as he had the misfortune, in music, to cross Wagner's path.

2

My second philosophical shock, a decade or so later, was my encounter with Auguste Comte, who led me in a radically different direction; it would be difficult to imagine two more dissimilar minds. If Comte had known Schopenhauer, he would probably have seen him merely as a metaphysician, in other words a representative of the past (estimable, no doubt, as Schopenhauer was a descendant of the 'greatest of metaphysicians', namely Kant; but a representative of the past all the same). If Schopenhauer had known Comte, he would probably not have taken his speculations very seriously. Incidentally, the two men were contemporaries (Schopenhauer's dates were 1788–1860, Comte's 1798–1860); quite often I am tempted to conclude that, intellectually speaking, nothing has happened since 1860. It is ultimately annoying to live in the middle of a period of mediocrities – especially when one feels incapable of raising the level. I doubt if I will produce any new philosophy; I think I would already have given some signs of this at my age; but I am pretty sure that I would produce better novels if the thinking around me were a little more inspiring.

Between Schopenhauer and Comte, I finally made my choice; and gradually, with a kind of disappointed enthusiasm, I became a positivist; to the same degree, I ceased to be a Schopenhauerian. Nevertheless, I nowadays rarely reread Comte, and never with a simple, immediate pleasure, but rather with the somewhat perverse pleasure (which can admittedly be really intense once you gain a taste for it) that one often derives from the stylistic quirks of unbalanced minds; but no philosopher, to my knowledge, is so immediately agreeable and reinvigorating to read as Arthur Schopenhauer. It is not even a matter of 'the art of writing', or any such nonsense; those are elementary rules that everyone should follow before having the nerve to propose their thought to the attention of the public. In his third *Untimely Consideration*, written shortly before he turned away from Schopenhauer, Nietzsche praised the latter's profound honesty, his probity, his uprightness; he speaks magnificently of his tone, that somewhat grumpy good humour which fills one with distaste for elegant writers and stylists. Such, in a broader form, is the purpose of this volume: I propose to show, through some of my favourite passages, why Schopenhauer's intellectual attitude remains to me a model for any future philosopher; and also why, even if you ultimately find yourself in disagreement with him, you cannot fail to be deeply grateful to him. For, to quote Nietzsche again, 'merely because such a man wrote, the burden of living on this Earth has been lightened.'

Chapter 1

The world is my representation

The world is my representation. This proposition is a truth for every living and thinking being, though only man can bring it to the state of abstract and reflective knowledge. When he really does so, one can say that the philosophical spirit has been born in him. He is then absolutely sure that he is acquainted with neither a sun nor an earth, but only with an eye that sees a sun, a hand which touches an earth.[1]

Schopenhauer was especially famous for his powerful depiction of the tragedy of the will, which has unfortunately had the effect of making him seem closer to the category of the novelists, or even worse that of the psychologists, and further removed from the 'true philosophers'. And yet there is in his work something that we won't find in Thomas Mann, let alone Freud: a complete philosophical system which aspires to answer all the questions (metaphysical, aesthetic, ethical) that have been asked by philosophy ever since its origins.

'The world is my representation': as the first sentence of a book, it's difficult to find anything franker or more honest. Schopenhauer uses this first proposition as a springboard for the philosophical spirit: as we can see, for him philosophy does not arise from death. Later, he will agree that awareness of our death is a powerful spur to the search for truth, or at least to the publication of works claiming that such is their aim (indeed, this awareness is a spur to pretty much every activity); but the main origin of all philosophy is the awareness of a gap, of an uncertainty about our knowledge of the world. Schopenhauer's philosophy is first and foremost a commentary on the conditions of knowledge – an epistemology.

Our own body is already an object, and, from this point of view, a representation. It is indeed only an object among objects, subject to the laws that apply to objects; but it is an immediate object. Like every object of intuition, it is subject to the formal conditions of all knowledge, namely time and space, from which multiplicity proceeds. [2]

7

There is something comforting about envisioning our own body as an immediate object; and something disturbing about considering multiplicity, an inexhaustible source of misfortune in practice, as a consequence of the formal conditions of knowledge – especially when we know (and it will be the merit of the twentieth century to have established this) that these conditions are not as binding as Kant supposed.

On the contrary, gravity, although it knows no exception, must be classified as knowledge a posteriori, *contrary to the opinion of Kant who, in his* Metaphysical Foundations of Natural Science, *considers it as knowable* a priori.[3]

Today we are familiar with massless particles on which gravity does not act; we are familiar with non-Euclidean geometries, etc. In short, we have succeeded, at the cost of some effort, in going beyond the a priori conditions of knowledge according to Kant – those conditions which, in the latter's view, ruled out any metaphysics. Conditions do exist, defined by our brain; but they are also variable. Thus metaphysics has become, in a way, doubly impossible.

The way children (and the congenitally blind, once they have been operated on) learn to see; the way we see a single object in spite of the double sensation received by our eyes; the double vision and the double touching caused when our sensory organs have been displaced from their usual position; the perception of objects as upright while their image in the eye is upside down; the purely internal function which leads to the creation of a sense of colour via the separation of polarized lights (an activity of the eye); and finally the stereoscope – all these facts are solid and irrefutable arguments which establish that intuition is not merely sensory, but on the contrary intellectual, that is to say, it consists in knowing the cause from the effect by means of the understanding, and thus presupposes causality, from which all intuition, and therefore all experience, derives its primary and sole possibility. Causality cannot, therefore, be drawn from experience, as Hume's scepticism, which is here refuted, would have it.[4]

Somewhere in the world, an observer has the impression that a needle is moving on the dial of his measuring instrument; he deduces from this that the needle has moved on the dial of his measuring instrument; if in doubt, he consults another observer, who confirms the observation. Any modelling of the world starts out from these elements of immediate causality, and must, at journey's end, finish with them. On this level, Schopenhauer's argument hasn't changed: the notion of observation contains in itself not only time and space (a needle moves), but also, as is essential to go beyond internal sensation, the idea of causality (I have the impression that a needle moves, therefore a needle moves).

On the one hand realist dogmatism, which considers the representation as an effect of the object, seeks to separate the representation from the object, whereas they actually form a unity, and to create a being quite distinct from the representation, an object in itself, independent of the subject – something quite inconceivable, for every object presupposes the subject, and thus remains only a repre-sentation. Against this, scepticism, starting out from the same erroneous premises, argues that in the representation we have only the effect and not the cause, and so we can know only the action of objects as distinct from their being, an action which may have almost no resemblance to those objects. For scepticism, it would indeed be wrong in general to accept this, since on the one hand causality is deduced from experience, and on the other hand the reality of experience must rest on causality.

We must correct these two theories, firstly by pointing out that the representation and the object are one and the same thing;

and secondly that the being of the objects of intuition simply is their action: this is what constitutes their actual reality, and to seek the presence of the object apart from the representation of a subject, the being of things apart from their action, is a foolish and contradictory enterprise; for the knowledge of an object's mode of action exhausts the idea of this object as object, that is, as representation, since this knowledge leaves nothing else in it to know. In this sense, the world of intuition in time and space, which reveals itself to us in the limpid form of causality, is perfectly real, and perfectly in accordance with the way in which it gives itself, fully and without reserve: as a representation, linked to the law of causality. This is its empirical reality. On the other hand, causality exists only in the understanding and for the understanding, so that the real world, that is, the active world, is always conditioned by the understanding, and without it would be nothing. Not only for this reason, but also because no object can without contra-diction be conceived apart from the subject, we must refuse to allow the dogmatics, who define the reality of the external world by its independence from the subject, to entertain the very possibility of any such reality. The world of objects as a whole is and remains a representation, and therefore remains eternally and forever conditioned by the subject; that is to say, it has a transcendental ideality.[5]

In his *Tractatus*, Wittgenstein in his first period would say the same thing: 'The world is what happens.'[6] At this stage of his work (he was not yet thirty), Schopenhauer, who after all had already written two works (*On the Fourfold Root of the Principle of Sufficient Reason*, and 'On Vision and Colours'), had reached a perfectly lucid position: he had assimilated Kant's critical philosophy, of which he gives a clearer and more precise account, and the first pages of the *World as Will and Representation* are simply a – particularly lucid – synthesis of these early works.

Wittgenstein soberly concludes his treatise with the proposition: 'On what I cannot speak about, I am obliged to keep silent'.[7] Schopenhauer, on the contrary, at this point embarks on the second stage of his career, in which he will earn undying glory; he is going to speak about what we cannot speak about: he is going to speak about love, death, pity, tragedy and pain, and attempt to extend the spoken word to the world of singing. Boldly, and still without parallel among philosophers, he will enter the field of novelists, musicians and sculptors (who will reward him with their lasting recognition, and will always be comforted to have at their side such a serene and lucid companion). He will not do so without trembling, for the world of human passions is a repellent, often atrocious world, stalked by sickness, suicide and murder; but he will do so, and he will open up new lands to philosophy (lands unexplored before him, and barely explored since). He will become the philosopher of the will; and his first decision when entering this new field will be to adopt the approach, highly unusual for a philosopher, of aesthetic contemplation.

Chapter 2

Look at things attentively

When, animated by the power of the mind, we abandon the habitual way of considering things; when we cease to explain, by the light of the principle of reason in its different forms, the mutual relations between things, which always ultimately come down to their relation to our own will; when we no longer consider the where, when, why, and wherefore of things, but simply and solely their nature; when, furthermore, we no longer allow abstract thought or the principles of reason to occupy our consciousness; when, instead of all that, we give ourselves up to the intuition of all the power of our mind, sink entirely into it, letting our entire consciousness be filled with the peaceful contemplation of a directly present natural object – be it a landscape, a tree, a rock, a building, or any other object; from the moment, to use a suggestive expression, when we entirely 'lose ourselves' in this object, that is to say when we forget our self, our will, and exist only as a pure subject, as a clear mirror of the object, so that it is as if the object were alone, without anyone perceiving it, and we can no longer distinguish the intuition from the one who intuits, because the two merge so that the consciousness is entirely filled and absorbed by a single intuitive image; when, finally, the object has freed itself from any relation to something else, and the subject has freed itself from any relation to the will: then, what is known is no longer the particular thing, but the Idea, the eternal form, the immediate objecthood of the will at this level; and he who is grasped by this contemplation thereby ceases to be an individual, as the individual has disappeared in the moment of contemplation: he has become the pure subject of knowledge, delivered from the will, from pain and time.[1]

This description of limpid contemplation – the origin of all art – is itself so limpid that it is easy to forget its deeply innovative character. Before Schopenhauer, the artist was generally seen as someone who *manufactured* things – things that were admittedly difficult to manufacture, and of a special order, such as concertos, sculptures and plays – but it was still a matter of manufacture. This is, of course, a legitimate point of view – and Schopenhauer would be the last person to overlook the difficulties in conceiving and executing a work of art. (People these days sometimes try to get back to this idea in order to minimize art, to make it a little more harmless, as when novelists are considered as mere story tellers, and contemporary artists chatter about their craft.) But the original point, the generating point of all creation, is fundamentally quite different; it consists in an innate (and thus not teachable) disposition for a passive and, as it were, dumbstruck contemplation of the world. The artist is always someone who might just as well do nothing but immerse himself contentedly in the world and in the vague daydream associated with it. Today, when art has become accessible to the masses and generates considerable financial flows, this has very comical consequences. Thus, the ambitious and enterprising individual with a range of social skills who nurses the ambition to *have a career* in art will rarely succeed; the palm will always go to pathetic blob-like folk who everyone initially thought were just losers. Thus also the publisher (or the producer, or the gallerist, or other indispensable intermediary), having brought an artist under his aegis, and being vaguely aware of the preceding truths, will always be prone to

16

a kind of anxiety. How can he ensure that his artist will continue to produce? The artist is certainly susceptible to money, to fame and to women; you can keep a grip on him through these things; but what lies at the origin of his art, makes it possible and ensures its success, is of a very different nature. Embarrassed by this truth, which all by itself ruined his philosophy, Nietzsche tried to ignore it by pleading palpable counter-truths: the poet has always been, he says, essentially driven by the desire to win the prize awarded to the best poet. Bullshit. No poet worthy of the name has ever refused the homage of an honour, a female suitor in a state of sexual arousal, or the sum of money that accompanies large sales; but neither has any artist been so foolish as to believe that the power of his desires could be related to the power of his work; this really would be to confuse the essential with the inessential. The inessential thing is that the poet is like other men (and, if he were really original, his creation would have little value); the essential thing is that, alone among grown-up men, he retains a faculty of pure perception which is usually met only in childhood, madness, or in the subject matter of dreams.

As we have said, the ordinary man, that industrial product of nature, something she manufactures in her thousands every day, is incapable – at least in a sustained manner – of that purely disinterested perception which constitutes contemplation: he can focus his attention on things only to the extent that they have a relationship, even very indirect, with his own will. From this point of view, which requires only the knowledge of the relations between things, the abstract concept of the thing is sufficient and usually indeed more useful; therefore, the ordinary man does not dwell long on pure intuition, and does not fix his gaze on an object for long; on the contrary, faced with all that is presented to him, he will quickly look for the concept under which he can categorize it, just as the lazy person looks for a chair, and then ceases to be interested in it.[2]

This passage incidentally explains why critical excellence is as rare in artistic matters as excellence is in producing works of art – and why it is basically of the same order. A work of art, in Schopenhauer's conception, is a kind of product of nature; it must share with nature a simplicity of purpose, an innocence; the critic must contemplate it with the same thoughtful and innocent attention that the artist gives to natural creations; if he fulfils this condition, his criticism will itself be a work of art. (It will be observed that the use of existing works of art in a new work has always been achieved without any difficulty; old works enter the new just as easily as do observations directly taken from life; there is no discontinuity here, no gap.) If, on the contrary, the critic seeks the concept to which he can reduce the work, if he seeks to *situate* it, to locate it by means of comparisons, contrasts or references, if he considers it (to speak in Schopenhauerian terms) from the point of view of relationship, then he will miss its essential nature.

Let us transport ourselves to a very solitary region, with a boundless horizon, under a cloudless sky: trees and plants in the still air, no animals, no men, no rivers or streams, the deepest silence; such an environment is like a summons to seriousness, to a contemplation detached from willing and its mediocre demands; this is what gives such a bare, deserted and profoundly peaceful landscape a touch of sublimity. Indeed, because it provides no object for the strivings and the mediocre expectations involved in willing, offers nothing that is favourable or unfavourable to them, it leaves only the possibility of pure contemplation.[3]

On the aesthetic level, as on many others, Nietzsche's thought is the exact opposite of Schopenhauer's. Indeed, Nietzsche goes to the ridiculous length of giving a general meaning to Stendhal's famous words 'Beauty is a promise of happiness', which obviously relate to female beauty, so that Stendhal could have written, more precisely, 'Eroticism is a promise of happiness.'

The feeling of the sublime arises from the fact that a thing directly unfavourable to the will becomes the object of a pure contemplation, which can be maintained only by constantly turning away from the will and rising above its interests; this is what comprises the sublimity of this state of consciousness. The pretty,[4] on the other hand, pulls the viewer out of the state of pure contemplation necessary to the conception of the beautiful by presenting him with immediately pleasant objects, thereby necessarily arousing the will, and forcing him to leave the state of being a pure subject of knowledge to turn him into an enslaved, dependent subject of willing. The concept of the pretty, which ordinarily applies to all that is cheerfully beautiful, has, for lack of a clear distinction, been excessively extended, and I consider it necessary to leave it aside. In the sense that I have just explained, I find in the field of art only two kinds of the pretty, which are both unworthy of it. The first, very inferior kind is found in the still lifes of the Dutch painters, when they stray so far as to represent edibles in such a realistic way that they merely provoke the appetite; this is obviously a stimulation of the will that puts an end to all aesthetic contemplation of the object. Fruit is still admissible, if it is presented as a development of the flower and as a product of nature, beautiful in form and colour, without our being directly obliged to think of its edible properties; unfortunately, we often find, painted with artless realism, dishes prepared and ready to eat such as oysters, herring, lobsters, slices of bread and butter, beer, wine, etc., which is altogether reprehensible. In the painting of history and sculpture, the pretty consists of nudes whose pose, in negligee, and the general way of depicting them tend to excite lust in the viewer; this at once brings aesthetic contemplation to an end and goes against the purpose of art. This failing corresponds exactly to what we have just pointed out in Dutch painters. The ancients, in spite of the beauty and the complete nudity of their statues, almost always avoid this, as the artist created them in an objective spirit filled with ideal beauty, not in a subjective spirit tainted by base desires. The pretty must therefore always be avoided in art.

There is also a negative pretty, which is even more reprehensible than the positive pretty we have just been speaking about: this is the repellent. Like the pretty in the proper sense, it awakens the viewer's will and thereby suppresses pure aesthetic contemplation. But this negative pretty arouses a violent repulsion, a disgust: it awakens the will by presenting objects that fill it with horror. It has long been recognized, therefore, that it is not admissible in art, although the ugly itself, as long as it is not repellent, can find its proper place in it.[5]

This definitive condemnation of the kind of things found in splatter films poses a difficult but unavoidable problem, for although tragedy very often – indeed, almost necessarily – calls for atrocious crimes, it has been very hesitant about whether these could be represented on stage; and it has, in most cases, concluded in the negative, as if the feeling of pity, constitutive of the tragic emotion, risked being blurred by too violent a sensory participation.

Similarly, while we can readily concede to Schopenhauer that the awakening of sexual desire in the viewer (what is called *eroticism*) is directly contrary to the object of art, the fact remains that the representation of human nudity is one of its most traditional subjects; and the representation of the sexual act itself (*pornography*) could belong to the artistic field if this could be achieved in an objective way, that is to say without awakening desire (or indeed repulsion). The distinction here is at once real, easy to test out (there is nothing more observable than an erection) and very difficult to conceptualize. Some cases are simple, and Schopenhauer points them out (a suggestive negligee, a lascivious pose or expression in the model); in other cases, it is the 'general way of depicting' nudity that creates a difference as subtle as it is irrefutable.

Since, on the one hand, every present thing can be considered in a purely objective way, irrespective of any relation; and since, on the other hand, the will, on some level of its objecthood, is manifested in every thing, so that this thing is the expression of an Idea; it follows that every thing is beautiful.[6]

After the art of the twentieth century, the 'viewer who creates the painting', and Duchamp's ready-mades, this idea strikes us as less surprising; when Schopenhauer formulated it, it was so radically new that its contemporaries do not even seem to have noticed it. It must be emphasized: for Schopenhauer, beauty is not a property belonging to certain objects of the world to the exclusion of others; so technical skill as such cannot produce its appearance; quite the contrary, it necessarily follows on *any* disinterested contemplation. This is something he expresses, even more bluntly, in these words: 'To say that a thing is beautiful is to express the fact that it is the object of our aesthetic contemplation.' No less clearly, he condemns the use of reflection and concepts in art.

Since the idea is and remains intuitive, the artist is not aware in abstract terms of the intention and purpose of his work; it is not a concept, but an idea that guides him; so he cannot give any explanation of his way of doing things: he works, as we say, unconsciously, 'by feeling', in truth instinctively.[7]

Peaceful contemplation, detached from all thought and all desire, of all the objects of the world: this is Schopenhauer's aesthetic, as simple as it is profoundly original, as far removed from classicism as from romanticism. Such a conception does not really belong to Western cultural history, and we can here see a first sign that Schopenhauer is getting closer to the 'deepest thought', the one which will lead him, as Nietzsche said, to 'make the threat of a new Buddhism hover over the West'.

This simple remark about the primacy of intuition also has interesting practical consequences. On the one hand, it indicates the limits of the interest that can be accorded to *interviews* with artists; if these artists are endowed with a rich conceptual imagination (and this is sometimes the case), they can amuse themselves by inventing this or that interpretation of their work; but they will never take the exercise altogether seriously. It indicates above all the very narrow limits within which the teaching of art must be confined; the personal study of the Old Masters is at bottom the only worthwhile exercise, and one can even dispense with that. If we follow Schopenhauer, the best possible way of reforming art schools would simply be to close them. The same is true, in his view, of the teaching of philosophy, and the connection is significant. For if Schopenhauer often argues his case, if his exceptional intelligence makes him capable of arguments as brilliant as the topic requires, the core of his philosophy, its true generating principle, does not belong to the realm of the concept; on the contrary, it resides in a single and essentially artistic intuition that probably came to him as early as the mid-1810s.

Chapter 3

In this way the will to live objectifies itself

When we consider things attentively, when we see the powerful, irresistible impulse with which waterfalls rush to the depths of the Earth, how the magnet always turns to the magnetic pole and iron rushes towards the magnet; when we note the violence with which two electric poles try to unite, a violence further intensified by obstacles, as are human desires; when we observe the suddenness of crystallization and its regularity, which is merely the abrupt cessation of a movement in different directions, a movement subject, when it solidifies, to rigorous laws; when we notice the way in which bodies released from the solid state and returned to the freedom of the fluid state seek each other or flee each other, unite or separate; when, finally, we notice how a burden whose attraction towards the Earth is blocked by our body weighs down and presses continually on that body in its attempt to follow its own course; then we will not need any great stretch of imagination to recognize, albeit from a great distance, our own essence, the very same essence which, within ourselves, pursues its goals enlightened by knowledge, but which here, in the weakest of its manifestations, strives blindly, dully and invariably, and which nevertheless, because it is everywhere one and the same – as the first light of dawn shares the name of sunlight with the full brightness of noon – must here too bear the name of will, which refers to the being of every thing in the world and the unique core of every phenomenon.[1]

This passage is typical of Schopenhauer's artistic manner; he sets out to make us feel an analogy which has been revealed to him by prolonged and profound contemplation. But it could all be done in exactly the opposite way. Consider the spontaneous, innocent, quite instinctive desire which attracts us to a girl with a nice figure; then, on the contrary, observe the involuntary recoil that paralyses us in the presence of danger, the fear that grips us at the prospect of physical pain: how can we not recognize, mediated by reason, and rendered accessible and expressible by language, the elementary powers of natural forces, acting eternally and invariably?

This is no more an anthropomorphization of the world than it is a mechanization of human passions; it is a matter of recognizing what is identical beyond the appearances, and justifying the main audacious stroke on which the whole system rests, namely the use of introspection as a method of metaphysical investigation.

Spinoza says (letter 62) that a stone hurled into the air would, if it were conscious, have the impression of moving of its own will. I will merely add that the stone would be right. The impetus is for the stone what a motive is for me, and what appears in it as cohesion, gravity and persistence is in its intimate nature the same thing that I recognize in myself as will – something that it too would recognize as will if it were endowed with knowledge. [2]

'Everything endeavours to persist in its own being,' says Spinoza. This passage highlights the extreme generality of Schopenhauer's notion of will, and how important it is to approach it without psychologism.

If Comte had been told about the metaphysics of willing developed by his German contemporary, the French philosopher would undoubtedly have seen it as a surprising return of fetishism – a radical fetishism, indeed, since, as Comte notes, drawing on Adam Smith, 'in no country, among no people, can we find any god of gravity'. To the early Comte, such an event would have seemed a curious counterexample to his analysis of historical movement; in his last years, on the other hand, he seemed more and more tempted by the idea of a return to fetishism, which alone was capable of serving as the basis for a new religion, since it alone could produce a sentimental attachment. The 'Great Fetish', however (to use Comte's picturesque name for the world), was very far from seeming so attractive to Schopenhauer. A religion can very well survive by pure force of terror (this is the case with all monotheisms). Such was not, however, Comte's aim; but it is also fair to point out that his last years were marked by intense but somewhat unfocused intellectual activity; in his work, there was not enough time for the religious synthesis to be fully worked out.

Indeed, the absence of any goal and any limit is essential to the will in itself, which is an endless striving. This, which has already been mentioned above in the case of centrifugal force, is also manifested in its simplest form at the lowest degree of objecthood of the will, namely gravity, whose constant striving, joined to the impossibility of reaching an ultimate goal, is clear to see. Suppose that all matter, in accordance with its will, were to clump together in a compact mass; gravity striving toward the centre would still struggle with impenetrability, in the form of rigidity or elasticity. The striving of matter can only be impeded, never realized or satisfied. So is it with the strivings of all manifestations of the will; every goal attained is the beginning of a new career, and this process has no end. The plant raises its manifestations from the seed to the stem, to the leaf, to the flower, to the fruit, and this is only the beginning of a new seed, a new individual that will, however, pursue the same old course, and so on for all eternity. The same applies to the life of animals: procreation is its culminating point, after which the life of the first individual fades away more or less quickly, while a new individual ensures the perpetuation of the species and repeats the same phenomenon. The constant renewal of the body's matter must also be seen as a manifestation of these continual drives and changes; physiologists no longer see it simply as a necessary renewal of the matter consumed by movement, as the possible wear and tear to the machine cannot be as great as the constant influx of food. An eternal becoming, an endless flow: these are the manifestations of the nature of willing. The same thing is unceasingly displayed in human endeavours and desires, whose realization is always dangled before us as the ultimate goal of our will; as soon as they are satisfied they are no longer recognized, they are soon forgotten, like something antiquated – and, truth to tell, even if we hide this fact from ourselves, we cast them aside as vanished illusions. Happy indeed is the man who still has desires and aspirations: he can continue from desire to its satisfaction, and from thence to another desire; when this movement is fast, it means happiness, and unhappiness when it is slow. At least he will not fall into a dreadful, paralysing stagnation, a dull desire with no definite object, a deadly languor.[3]

Schopenhauer has too often been likened to Baltasar Gracián, or the French moralists – and it is true that he himself sometimes encouraged this comparison. Many of his best passages, in fact, are more reminiscent of a commentary on Ecclesiastes 1:8: 'All things are full of labour; man cannot utter it.' It is not only, or even especially, human activity that is a form of vanity: nature, the whole of nature, is an endless striving, without purpose or respite: 'All is vanity and vexation of spirit' (Ecclesiastes 1:14). It is easy to see how inadequate Schopenhauer would have found twentieth-century conceptions of the absurd: for him, the most telling example of this absurdity is the incessant work of gravity. The absurdity of man's fate does not appear to

31

be particularly shocking, unless we on principle attribute a transcendent value to human existence, for instance by adopting a Christian or, at a pinch, a political point of view; nothing is further from Schopenhauer's thought.

If it is the world as a whole that is unacceptable, it is quite legitimate to feel a particular contempt for life. Not just for 'human life'; for all life. Animal life is not only absurd, it is atrocious. 'What an execrable thing is this nature of which we are part!' exclaims Schopenhauer, in the wake of Aristotle. The following passage, with its immense final sentence, so deep – as deep as the abyss, majestic in its desolation and horror – is one of those that can provoke a stupefaction, a final *coming to awareness*, like a lightning crystallization of the scattered feelings left in us by the experience of life; it is difficult to imagine anyone, at any moment in history, adding a single word to it. I wish to dedicate it especially to ecologists.

It is, however, in the life of animals, so simple and easy to survey, that the vanity and nothingness of the strivings of the whole phenomenon can be grasped. The diversity of organizations, the perfection of the means by which each one is adapted to its environment and its prey, contrast vividly *with the absence of any enduring goal; instead of this goal there is a moment of pleasure, so fleeting, which is inseparable from need, countless prolonged sufferings, an incessant struggle,* bellum omnium, *in which each is both hunter and prey, tumult, privation, misery and fear, shouts and screams, this is what appears to us; and so it will continue,* in secula seculorum, *or until the crust of the planet again bursts open. Junghuhn recounts how in Java he saw a stretch of ground covered with bones, extending as far as the eye could see, that he took for a battlefield: these were actually just the skeletons of large turtles, five feet long, three feet wide and tall; when they leave the sea, these turtles take this path to lay their eggs, and are then assaulted by wild dogs (*Canis rutilans*) *which combine their efforts to tip them onto their backs, tear off the lower carapace and the small scales on their bellies, and devour them alive. But a tiger often then pounces on the dogs. This desolation is renewed thousands and thousands of times, year after year; it is for this purpose that these turtles are born. For what fault must they endure such a torment? Why these scenes of horror? There is only one answer: in this way the will to live objectifies itself.*[4]

Chapter 4

The theatre of the world

Many of the most impressive metaphors in Schopenhauer (and, indeed, in the whole of literature) are borrowed from the world of theatre. On a stage, the world as representation is reduced to its simplest expression; the scenery, unrealistic in principle, cannot become an object of aesthetic contemplation; it can be reduced to nothing without any noticeable inconvenience; when it does exist, it has no other function than to highlight the real stake of the play, namely the conflict of passions.

When he withdraws into reflection, man resembles an actor who has just performed his scene and, while waiting for the next, takes his seat among the spectators, from where he contemplates the unfolding of the action, even if this involves the preparations for his death, before returning to act and suffer, as he must.[1]

This emphasis on staging is mainly used when it comes to highlighting the artificial, symbolic nature of the theatre; and in fact, systems of morality based on reason are somewhat artificial. In the last pages of Part I of the *World as Will and Representation*, Schopenhauer deals with those (the Stoics) who sought to found morality, and the principles of conduct in life, on the use of reason; here is the conclusion to his examination:

The fundamental contradiction under which Stoic ethics labours is even clearer from the fact that its ideal, the Stoic sage, is described in a way deprived of any life or poetic truth; he remains a stiff, inert manikin; we do not know what to make of him, and he himself does not know what to do with his wisdom; his calm, contentment and happiness are so opposed to human nature that we cannot even form an intuitive representation of him.[2]

The condemnation is all the more striking in that Schopenhauer himself, in his 'Aphorisms on the Wisdom of Life', would end up dispensing practical advice quite similar to that of the Stoics. It is true that this latter work, presupposing the existence of a happy life, rests on a compromise; in order to write it, Schopenhauer had 'to depart entirely from the elevated metaphysical and moral point of view to which [my] real philosophy leads'. This excerpt constitutes a second and no less important restriction on the notion of *Lebenweisheit*. The argument employed is also striking: what condemns the Stoic sage, and what renders his existence unlikely, is the *absence of poetic truth* in such a character; no philosopher until then had taken poetry so seriously.

It is the subject of willing, that is to say, his own will, which fills the consciousness of the lyrical author, often as a free and satisfied willing (joy), but much more often as a frustrated willing (sadness), and always as an emotion, a passion, a state of mind. Yet, alongside and at the same time as this state, the glances that the poet casts on the nature all around him make him aware of himself as a pure subject of knowledge, independent of willing, whose imperturbable spiritual peace contrasts with the desires of the ever-pressured, ever-greedy will: the feeling of this contrast, of this alternation, is expressed in the genre of lyric poems, and constitutes in short the lyrical state of mind. In this state, pure knowledge comes to us to deliver us from willing and its torments: we surrender ourselves to it, but only for a moment; ever and again the will, and the memory of our personal goals, comes to tear us away from peaceful contemplation; but again and again the beauty of our surroundings, through which a knowledge liberated from willing is offered to us, comes to seduce us. That is why, in song and lyrical inspiration, the will (self-interested and personal views) and the pure intuition of our surroundings are admirably mixed: reconciliations between the two are sought out and imagined; the subjective disposition of mind, the affection of willing, plays a part in the intuition of the surrounding world, and reciprocally lends its colours to it: the true lyric poem is the imprint of these mixed and shared states of mind.[3]

To this luminous analysis, I can find just one thing to add: it is only quite recently (in the middle of the nineteenth century in Paris – Baudelaire was the first to perceive it; it certainly happened later in Germany) that urban poetry became possible. It is only quite recently that the city became extensive enough to constitute such a vast, anonymous environment, with its sometimes grandiose, sometimes appalling beauty, unlikely to present to the poet's consciousness anything connected to his will, but ultimately likely to remain as foreign to him as nature at its wildest. The one difference is that the tranquillity afforded by the contemplation of the urban landscape must be conquered in a bitter struggle, and in the midst of even more acute suffering.

The description of a great misfortune is the only indispensable element in tragedy. The many different ways in which the poet introduces this description can be reduced to three types. First of all, it can come through the exceptional malice, bordering on the limits of the possible, of some character who will be the architect of the misfortune; examples of this kind are Richard III, Iago in Othello, *Shylock in* The Merchant of Venice, *Franz Moor, Euripides'* Phaedra, *Creon in* Antigone, *and many others. It can also come about by means of blind fate, that is, by chance and error: Sophocles'* Oedipus Rex *is a true example of this type, as is* The Women of Trachis, *and generally speaking most ancient tragedies; among the modern ones we might mention* Romeo and Juliet, *Voltaire's* Tancred *and* [Schiller's] The Bride of Messina. *Finally, misfortune can be brought about by the simple situation of the characters with respect to each other, by their circumstances; there is no need either for a monstrous error, or for an extraordinary fate, or for a character at the limits of human wickedness; on the contrary, characters familiar to us from the moral point of view, and placed in ordinary circumstances, find themselves in situations which force them to prepare for each other, in full knowledge and in full awareness, the most horrendous misfortunes, without the fault being clearly attributable to any one of the parties. This last method appears greatly preferable to the two others because it does not show us the most extreme misfortune as an exception, nor as something which is brought about by exceptional circumstances or monstrous characters, but as something which comes about easily, as it were of itself and almost necessarily, from the conduct and character of men, and thereby brings it terrifyingly close to us.*[4]

Schopenhauer indicates a little further on that this method, which seems to him the best, is also the most difficult, and he struggles to cite a convincing example. Curiously, the situation has not changed much. Even if we no longer believe in gods who play with our destinies 'like a backgammon player', we still believe in Fate; indeed, fantastic literature, which has developed a great deal since Schopenhauer's time, makes essential use of it. As for characters of an 'exceptional malice, bordering on the limits of the possible', there have been several embodiments of them, in modern times too. The tragedy of banality, produced by ordinary circumstances, and therefore all the more inescapable, remains to be written.

Chapter 5

The conduct of life: what we are

In addition to its lofty mission of presenting us with an overall representation of the world compatible with the state of the sciences, a representation that is accessible to intuition and satisfying for reason, philosophy traditionally has another function: to provide us with advice applicable to the conduct of life, to help us to achieve 'wisdom' in the practical sense. In Schopenhauer's case, the trouble is that the first function makes the second impossible; in fact, his philosophy leads to quite simple conclusions: the world is an unfortunate thing, and it would be better if it did not exist; inside the world, the universe of living things constitutes an area of intensified suffering; and human life, its most complete form, is also the most painful. Such a philosophy is deeply consoling; it helps to cut off the roots of envy, that fertile source of human misfortunes: all enjoyment, however desirable it may seem, is in fact relative, obtained only at the cost of immense effort, and doomed to come to a rapid end. It is a philosophy that also helps us to accept death, above all by presenting non-being as the extinction of suffering. On the other hand, it is extremely poor in practical consequences: if life really is pain, then the best thing to do, it seems, is to stay quietly in one's corner while waiting to grow old and die, which will solve all our problems. Schopenhauer was intensely aware of all this as he began writing the 'Aphorisms on the Wisdom of Life'.

I take the notion of wisdom in life here in its purely immanent sense – that is, I understand it to mean the art of organizing one's life as pleasantly and happily as possible; advice for this purpose could be called eudaemonology: it would thus be a method for attaining a happy life. This could be defined as an existence which, considered objectively, or rather (because this is a matter of subjective appreciation), on cool and careful reflection, would be decidedly preferable to non-existence. From this notion it follows that we would be attached to this existence for itself, and not simply out of fear of death, and furthermore that we would wish to see it last indefinitely. Whether human life corresponds to the notion of such an existence, or ever could correspond to it, is a question to which, as is well known, my philosophy answers in the negative, whereas eudaemonology presupposes an affirmative answer. This latter doctrine is based precisely on the innate error that I denounce in chapter 49 of volume 2 of my main work. Nevertheless, to work on this subject, I have had to stray entirely from the elevated metaphysical and moral point of view to which my true philosophy leads. Consequently, the whole of the following analysis rests, in a way, on an accommodation, in the sense that it simply adopts the usual, empirical point of view, and preserves the error within it. Its value can thus only be conditional, and the word eudaemonology itself is only a euphemism.[1]

Why, then, did he embark on such an enterprise? It's hard to say, but the fact is that we would miss this book, which is certainly the most brilliant, the most accessible and the funniest he ever wrote. In fact, having absolved himself of the need to be consistent from the very first page, Schopenhauer here gives us a series of profound, sensitive insights, incredibly free in tone, into what exactly we can expect from human existence. If he remains convinced that the best thing would be to get rid of desire completely, resulting in a peaceful life that can be summed up as waiting for death, he knows that the task is not easy and, rather than simply cutting off desire, he proposes a series of sensible ways for weakening it. The message is still the radical message of Buddhism; but it's basically a Buddhism that has been tempered, humanized, adapted to our culture, to our impatient and greedy temperament, to our feeble capacity for renunciation. From this comes the book's easy and affable aspect, from which it is very difficult to extract passages, as everything is linked together with such limpidity and brio – we feel that the author, forsaking for a time the arduous peaks of metaphysics, is having fun with an elementary and not altogether serious subject, namely human life. It is also a book to which one generally does not wish to add the slightest comment, as its veracity is best preserved intact. Metaphysics has changed, because physics itself has changed; but human life is still played out according to pretty much the same rules, and one can see this as a melancholy confirmation of the lines with which Schopenhauer concludes his introduction.

In general, it is true that the sages of all times have always said the same thing, and the fools, that is to say, the immense majority in all times, have always done the same thing, that is, the opposite; and it will ever be thus. Voltaire also says, 'We will leave this world as stupid and as wicked as we found it when we arrived.'[2]

As everything that exists and occurs for man exists and occurs immediately only in and for his consciousness, it is obviously the nature of this consciousness which will be first and foremost the essential thing, and in most cases everything will depend on this, more than on the shapes represented in it. All splendour, all enjoyment, are poor when they take place in the dull consciousness of a fool, in comparison with the consciousness of Cervantes when, in the discomfort of jail, he wrote his Don Quixote.

The objective half of actuality and reality lies in the hands of fate, and is thus changeable; the subjective half is ourselves, so it is essentially unchangeable. Thus each man's life, in spite of all external changes, has on average an unchanging character, and can be compared to a series of variations on one and the same theme. Nobody can escape from his individuality. And it is the same for a man as for an animal: whatever the conditions in which we place him, he remains trapped in the narrow circle that nature has irrevocably drawn for his being, which explains, for example, why our efforts to make happy a loved animal must, because of these limits in its being and its consciousness, necessarily remain within very restricted limits; man also has his possibilities of happiness fixed in advance by his individuality. In particular, the limits of his intellectual power determine once and for all his aptitude for elevated enjoyment. If these limits are narrow, all external efforts, everything that men or fortune can do for him, will be powerless to transport him above the mass of usual human (and half-animal) happiness: he will have to content himself with sensual enjoyments, an intimate and cheerful family life, low company and vulgar hobbies. Even education cannot do much, if anything, to expand this circle. Indeed, the highest, the most varied, and the most enduring pleasures are those of the mind, although we were so wrong about this in our youth; these pleasures depend above all on the innate power of our mind. It is therefore easy to see how much our happiness depends on who we are, on our individuality, whereas most of the time we take into account only our fate, what we have, or what we represent. Fate can improve; and when someone possesses inner wealth, he will not expect much from it; but until the end of his days a fool remains a fool, a moron remains a moron, even if he is in paradise and surrounded by houris.[3]

The final comments here may seem surprising, as well as the use of the general term 'enjoyments' (*Genüsse*). It is easy to agree that a moron is largely unable to enjoy the beauties of a symphony or a subtle piece of reasoning; this is more surprising in the case of, say, fellatio; and yet experience confirms it. The richness of pleasure, even sexual pleasure, resides in the intellect, and it is directly proportional to the power of the latter; unfortunately, the same is true of pain.

It is not without sadness that we hear of the simple joys of the ordinary man (an intimate and cheerful family life, run-of-the-mill friends), since in our modern societies they really appear as a *paradise lost*: even sensual pleasures are declining. And if all these pleasures are decreasing, they are certainly not being replaced by the 'elevated enjoyment' of the mind, but rather by the striving for what Schopenhauer considers a mere illusion: money and fame (what we have, what we represent). We will have the opportunity to come back to these two phenomena; but such an observation is already enough to condemn modern society.

That the subjective is incomparably more essential to our happiness and our enjoyment than the objective can be

46

confirmed by everything, from the hunger that is the best of sauces and the indifference with which the old man considers the goddess that the young man idolizes, to the life of the genius and the saint. Health, above all, is so much more important than all external goods that, in truth, a healthy beggar is happier than a sick king. A calm and serene temperament, based on perfect health and a happy organization, a lucid, lively, penetrating and right-thinking reason, a tempered and gentle will that produces a good conscience, these are advantages that no wealth, no rank can replace. What a man is for himself, what keeps him company in solitude and that no one can give him or take from him, is obviously more important to him than what he can possess, or what he can be in the eyes of others. A man of wit, even in the deepest solitude, will find in his own thoughts and fantasies a perfect distraction, while the continual change brought about by society, plays, excursions and parties will be quite unable to ward off the boredom that tortures the fool. A good, moderate, peaceful character may be satisfied in indigence, while no amount of riches can satisfy an avid, envious, and wicked character.[4]

The most extreme and demanding form of courage, writes Chesterton in *Heretics*, consists in climbing a tower to assert to the assembled crowd that two and two make four. He himself did not always have this courage, and often preferred, as is natural, to spin out ingenious, innovative or brilliant insights. Schopenhauer was writing for eternity (without paying any attention to the prejudices of his time, either to consolidate them or to combat them), writing as if his book alone were to survive and to contain all human wisdom, so he found the energy necessary to utter banalities and commonplaces when he thought they were correct; he systematically placed truth above originality; for an individual of his calibre, this was doubtless far from easy.

But what, above all, makes us most immediately happy is cheerfulness of soul, for this good quality immediately finds its reward in itself. Indeed, that which is cheerful is always right to be so, in that it is cheerful. Nothing can replace all other goods as much as this quality, while it cannot itself be replaced by anything. Let a man be young, handsome, rich and esteemed; let us ask, if we wish to gauge his happiness, if he is cheerful. And if, on the other hand, he is cheerful, it does not matter whether he is young or old, straight-backed or hunchbacked, poor or rich: he is happy. In my early years, I opened an old book one day and read: 'He who laughs a lot is happy, he who cries a lot is unhappy' – a very naive remark, but because of its simple truth I could not forget it, although it is the superlative of a truism. And so, every time that cheerfulness presents itself, we must open our doors and windows to it.

In the dark and lucid philosophy of Schopenhauer, there is little room for candid cheerfulness. However, he does sometimes note, with surprise, the existence of those little moments of unforeseen happiness, those little miracles.

Most splendours are pure illusions, like a stage set, and the essence of the thing is lacking. Thus, ships festooned with pennants and wreaths, cannon shots, drums and trumpets, cries of exultation, shouts of joy, and so forth: all this is the advertisement, the indication, the hieroglyph of joy; but most often joy herself is not there: she alone has sent her excuses for not coming to the party. Where she really presents herself, she usually comes without being invited or announced, of herself and without ceremony, introducing herself in silence, often for the most insignificant and trivial reasons, in the most mundane circumstances, on occasions that are far from brilliant or glorious. [5]

An overall survey shows us that the two enemies of human happiness are suffering and boredom. We can also remark that, to the extent that we succeed in moving away from the one, we approach the other, and reciprocally; our lives actually represent an oscillation, strong or weak, between the two. This stems from the fact that both are in a double antagonism towards each other; the first is external, or objective; the second is internal, or subjective. Indeed, outwardly, need and deprivation cause suffering; conversely, security and overabundance give rise to boredom. In accordance with this we see the lower classes immersed in an incessant combat against need, and thus pain, while on the contrary the wealthy upper classes conduct an incessant, often desperate struggle against boredom.[6] Internal or subjective antagonism is based on the fact that, in every individual, receptivity to boredom is in inverse ratio to his receptivity to suffering, which is determined by the measure of his intellectual powers. In fact, a dull mind always goes hand in hand with a dull sensibility and a lack of excitability, which render the individual less receptive to all kinds and degrees of pain and sadness; but this same dullness of the mind also produces what is depicted on so many faces, and is revealed by an attention forever alert to all the events, however insignificant, of the external world – that inner emptiness which is the true source of boredom, and which continually craves external stimulation, anything that can set the heart and mind in motion.[7]

As all the external sources of happiness and pleasure are, by their nature, highly uncertain, doubtful, ephemeral, and subject to chance, they dry up in certain circumstances; moreover, this is inevitable, as they cannot always be at hand. In old age, they almost all inevitably decline; for it is then that we are abandoned by love, banter, the pleasures of travelling and horse riding, as well as the aptitude to play a part in the world, and even by our friends and relatives who are taken from us by death. It is then, more than ever, that there returns the question of knowing what every man has for himself, because that is what will last the longest. However, at any age, this is and remains the true and only permanent source of happiness. There is not much to be gained in this world: privation and suffering fill it, and for those who have avoided these, boredom lurks at every corner. Moreover, it is usually mediocrity that governs this world and foolishness that speaks out. Fate is cruel and men are wretched. In such a world, the man who has a great deal within himself shines like a room decorated for Christmas, bright, warm and cheerful amid the snows and ice of a December night. Therefore, to have a remarkable and rich individuality, and above all to have a superior mind, is undoubtedly the happiest fate on earth, however different it may be from the most brilliant fate.[8]

Against all this, however, we must also consider that the great gifts of the mind, as a result of the preponderance of nervous activity, produce an extreme increase in one's sensitivity to suffering in all its forms. Moreover, the passionate temperament which is their precondition, and the vivacity and the heightened state of all perception which are inseparable from them, produce an incomparably greater intensity, while there are far more painful than pleasant emotions; and finally, the great gifts of the mind alienate their possessor from other men and their activities, since the more he possesses in himself, the less he can find in them, and a hundred things which give them great satisfaction strike him as insipid and repellent; perhaps the law of compensation that holds sway everywhere also makes its presence felt in this area; has it not often been claimed, with some reason, that the man with the most limited mind was at bottom the happiest? Be that as it may, no one will envy him his happiness. [9]

Can we be so sure?

Chapter 6

The conduct of life: what we have

The question of whether or not elevated intellectual forces are favourable to human happiness may appear to be very theoretical, since in any case we cannot change them (either to increase them or even to limit them; there is no clear way of becoming a moron). It is not the same for fortune: we can increase our wealth, we can at least try; we can – in this case very easily – reduce it. On this point, it will be noted with satisfaction that Schopenhauer gives very clear advice.

I do not think I am doing anything unworthy of my pen by recommending here that one take good care of keeping his fortune, whether inherited or acquired. For to possess enough to be able, even if one is alone and without a family, to live comfortably in true independence, that is, without working, is a priceless advantage: it grants one exemption and immunity from the miseries and torment attached to human life, as well as emancipation from the general chores which are the natural fate of the children of the earth. It is only by this favour of fate that one is truly a free born man, and really sui juris *(his own master), master of his time and his powers, and able to say every morning: 'The day belongs to me'. Also, between the man who has a thousand pounds of income and the man who has a hundred thousand, the difference is infinitely less than between the former and the man who has nothing. But inherited wealth achieves its highest value when it falls to the one who, endowed with superior intellectual powers, pursues enterprises that are not really compatible with having to earn one's bread: he is then doubly favoured by fate and can live in full accord with his genius. He will pay his debt to humankind a hundred times over by producing what no one else could produce and giving it what will become its common good, while at the same time making it honourable. Another, placed in such a favoured position, will render himself worthy of humankind by his philanthropic works. Whoever, on the contrary, does nothing of this kind, who does not even try, if only once, as an experiment, to advance a science through serious studies, and does not give himself even the smallest opportunity of doing so, is merely a contemptible idler.*[1]

Notes

Preface: The history of a revolution

1 Michel Houellebecq, *The Possibility of an Island*, translated by Gavin Bowd (London: Weidenfeld, 2005).

2 Arthur Schopenhauer, *The World as Will and Representation*, edited and translated by Judith Norman, Alistair Welchman and Christopher Janaway, 2 vols (Cambridge: Cambridge University Press, 2010).

3 In Arthur Schopenhauer, *Parerga and Paralipomena: short philosophical essays*, edited and translated by Christopher Janaway, Sabine Roehr and Adrian Del Caro, 2 vols (Cambridge: Cambridge University Press, 2015–16), vol. 1, pp. 273–436. (As the translations of Schopenhauer by Houellebecq have such a vividly personal flavour, *all* the translations from *The World as Will and Representation*, and from *Parerga and Paralipomena*, in *In the Presence*

of Schopenhauer are based on the French versions by Houellebecq – and, in the case of the Preface, by Agathe Novak-Lechevalier – though I have also consulted the Cambridge University Press translations noted in notes 2 and 3 of the Preface and, where necessary, Schopenhauer's original German. Translator's note.)

4 See below, p. 2.

5 Michel Houellebecq, *Submission*, translated by Lorin Stein (London: William Heinemann, 2016), p. 7.

6 *Ibid.*

7 See the collection of Houellebecq's poetry, *Unreconciled: Poems 1991–2013*, translated by Gavin Bowd (London: William Heinemann, 2017). (Translator's note.)

8 Michel Houellebecq, *H. P. Lovecraft: Against the World, Against Life*, translated by Dorna Khazeni (London: Weidenfeld and Nicolson, 2006).

9 Michel Houellebecq, *Rester vivant: suivi de La poursuite du bonheur* (Paris: Flammarion, 1997).

10 Arthur Schopenhauer, *The World as Will and Representation*, Book 1, Chapter 56.

11 Houellebecq, *Rester vivant: suivi de La poursuite du bonheur*.

12 Schopenhauer, *The World as Will and Representation*, preface to the first edition.

13 Schopenhauer, *The World as Will and Representation*, Book 1, Chapter 38.

14 Michel Houellebecq, interview in *Le Point*, special issue, October–November 2016, p. 74.

15 Friedrich Nietzsche, 'Schopenhauer as Educator', in *Untimely Considerations*, edited by Daniel Breazeale, translated by R. J. Hollingdale (Cambridge: Cambridge University Press, 1997), p. 134.

16 *Ibid.*

17 *Ibid.*

18 Michel Houellebecq, *Interventions 2* (Paris: Flammarion, 2009), p. 153.

19 Michel Onfray, 'L'absolue singularité. Miroir du nihilisme', in Agathe Novak-Lechevalier (ed.), *Cahier de l'Herne Michel Houellebecq* (Paris: Herne, 2017), pp. 252–6.

20 See below, p. 4.

21 Michel Houellebecq, *The Map and the Territory*, translated by Gavin Bowd (London: Vintage, 2012). See also Pierre Dos Santos, 'Une éthique de la contemplation', in Novak-Lechevalier (ed.), *Cahier de l'Herne Michel Houellebecq*, pp. 222–5.

22 See below, pp. 3–4.

23 Michel Houellebecq, 'Approches du désarroi', in Houellebecq, *Interventions 2*, pp. 36–8.

24 *Ibid.*

25 *Ibid.*, p. 38.

26 *Ibid.*, p. 45.

Leave childhood behind, my friend, and wake up!

1 This quotation from Rousseau is the epigraph to the first book of *The World as Will and Representation*.

Chapter 1: The world is my representation

1 Arthur Schopenhauer, *The World as Will and Representation*, Book 1, Chapter 1.

2 *Ibid.*, Book 1, Chapter 2.

3 *Ibid.*, Book 1, Chapter 4.

4 *Ibid.*

5 *Ibid.*, Book 1, Chapter 5.

6 Houellebecq translates Wittgenstein's '*Die Welt ist alles, was der Fall ist*' as '*Le monde est ce qui arrive*'. A more common English translation is: 'The world is all that is the case.' (Translator's note.)

7 Houellebecq translates Wittgenstein's '*Wovon man nicht sprechen kann, darüber soll man schweigen*' as '*Sur ce dont je ne peux parler, j'ai l'obligation de me taire*'. A more common English translation is: 'That whereof one cannot speak, thereof one must be silent.' (Translator's note.)

Chapter 2: Look at things attentively

1 *The World as Will and Representation*, Book 3, Chapter 34.

2 *Ibid.*, Book 3, Chapter 36.

3 *Ibid.*, Book 3, Chapter 39.

4 Houellebecq uses '*le joli*' for Schopenhauer's '*das Reizende*', which can also be translated as 'the attractive', 'the stimulating', 'the alluring'. (Translator's note.)

5 *The World as Will and Representation*, Book 3, Chapter 40.

6 *Ibid.*

7 *Ibid.*, Book 3, Chapter 49.

Chapter 3: In this way the will to live objectifies itself

1 *The World as Will and Representation*, Book 2, Chapter 23.

2 *Ibid.*, Book 2, Chapter 24.

3 *Ibid.*, Book 2, Chapter 29.

4 Supplements to *The World as Will and Representation*, Chapter XXVIII. (In the Cambridge University Press edition – see note 2 to the Preface, above – this chapter is in vol. 2. Translator's note.)

Chapter 4: The theatre of the world

1 *The World as Will and Representation*, Book 1, Chapter 16.

2 *Ibid.*

3 *Ibid.*, Book 3, Chapter 51.

4 *Ibid.*

Chapter 5: The conduct of life: what we are

1 Schopenhauer, 'Aphorisms on the Wisdom of Life', Introduction.

2 *Ibid.*

3 *Ibid.*, Chapter 1.

4 *Ibid.*

5 *Ibid.*, Chapter 5, 1.

6 The life of nomads, representing the lowest degree of civilization, coincides with the highest degree, the life of the tourist, which has become universal. The first is caused by need, the second by boredom. (Schopenhauer's footnote.)

7 Schopenhauer, 'Aphorisms on the Wisdom of Life', Chapter 2.

8 *Ibid.*

9 *Ibid.*

Chapter 6: The conduct of life: what we have

1 Schopenhauer, 'Aphorisms on the Wisdom of Life', Chapter 3.